Table of Contents

French Bulldog Puppy Training 1

The Ultimate Guide on French Bulldog Puppies 1

What to Do When You Bring Home Your New French Bulldog Puppy 1

Limitation of Liability/Disclaimer 4

Bringing Home a New French Bulldog Puppy 6

Characteristics of Your French Bulldog Puppy 8

New French Bulldog Puppy Supplies You Must Have 11

Best Ways to Puppy Proof Your Home or Apartment 14

How to Socialize Your French Bulldog Puppy 17

How to Teach Your Puppy its Name 22

How to Teach Your Puppy to Sit, Stay and Come 26

How to Stop Puppy Whining 30

How to Stop Your French Bulldog Puppy from Biting 34

How to Stop Your Puppy from Jumping 37

How to Introduce a Collar and Leash to Your French Bulldog Puppy 39

How to Teach Your French Bulldog Puppy to Walk on a Leash 43

How to Crate Train a French Bulldog Puppy 46

How to Potty Train a New French Bulldog Puppy 49

The ABC's of How to Feed a French Bulldog Puppy Properly 52

How Much Should I Feed My New French Bulldog Puppy 55

Puppy Training - 7 Most Important Words Your French Bulldog Puppy Should Know 57

How to Brush Your Puppy's Teeth 60

The Right Way to Start Bathing Your New French Bulldog Puppy 64

Helpful Tips on Teething and the Need to Chew For Your Puppy 66

Puppy Identification Options 70

Puppy Air Travel -The Most Current Guidelines You May Not Know 72

Top 4 Reasons Why You Need Pet Insurance 75

How to Teach Your French Bulldog Puppy Tricks 78

How to Exercise Your French Bulldog 81

Vaccines Your French Bulldog Puppy Needs 83

A Puppy's 10 Commandments 86

Bringing Home a New French Bulldog Puppy

Bringing home a new French Bulldog puppy can be a fun and memorable time. It can also be a lot of work filled with a whole new set of responsibilities. This guide will help you maneuver through those first few weeks and months with your new best friend.

The first three months for a French Bulldog puppy is the most important time in their life. This is the window of time in a puppy's life that determines the type of dog they will become as an adult. This is when the dog's future temperament, character and behavior habits will be developed.

What you do right and what you do wrong with your puppy during this time period will affect their behavior forever.

In this book, you will learn everything you need to know so you can help your French Bulldog puppy grow into a happy, obedient and well mannered dog.

Topics covered include: what supplies you will need when they are first brought home, how to puppy proof your home so your puppy is safe, how to house train, what food to feed and how much, bathing tips, pros and cons of puppy insurance and more.

You will also learn the best ways to properly socialize your French Bulldog puppy, how to train it to sit, stay and come, how to help it learn its name fast, how to stop whining, biting and jumping up on people.

If you choose to crate train there is chapter on the best way to do this for your puppy.

When your puppy goes through teething this book will help you to be prepared on what to do.

The most current pet identification options and required vaccines will also be covered here.

Before you are finished you will learn games that you and your French Bulldog puppy will enjoy playing together, and the best ways to teach your new puppy tricks.

Finally, we will finish with a very poignant Puppies Ten Commandments.

You will find this a very helpful and thorough guide, essential to making sure the transition for you and your family and new French Bulldog puppy is as positive and successful as possible.

Characteristics of Your French Bulldog Puppy

The French Bulldog is a small, stout and energetic breed. Over the last few years it has been gaining in popularity. With its large expressive eyes, smooth coat that comes in many colors and small bat-like ears, it is hard to resist this adorable dog.

It has a great personality, is highly sociable, at times comical and well known for its ability to entertain for hours. With such a pleasant temperament along with its loyalty this makes the French Bull a great choice for a household pet. They are definitely not kennel dogs and prefer being around people.

Playful and at times hilarious in their antics, French Bulldogs can be a lot of fun. They like to run around, play games and chase after toys. Although they are very affectionate they can also be temperamental and may be better suited for older children.

They like to think they are lap dogs and that works well if you are okay sitting with a compact, muscular dog. They do have very soft outer coat.

They do not need much exercise but do enjoy a short walk each day. For this reason they make an excellent pet for those owners living in small dwellings or apartments. However, French Bulldogs love to eat and if not given enough exercise can pack on the pounds. An overweight French Bulldog will not be a healthy dog.

French Bulldogs can be stubborn and manipulative. When training you must show them you mean what you say through consistency and patience. They respond best to praise and food treats. Do not train with harsh measures as this will not work well with this breed. They have the tendency to bond very strongly to one person, in particular, and that person often makes the best trainer.

Similarly, house breaking can take a while with these dogs. Be aware that there will be mistakes and just have patience. You and your French Bulldog will eventually reach a point where everything begins to click.

You will want to give them proper socialization, early on, so they do well around other dogs. Around strangers they may have the tendency to bark at first and be a little reserve, but within a few minutes will warm up to people that are new.

They are easy to maintain and do not require much grooming. An occasional brushing with a rubber brush will do well to remove lose hair. As well, under the folds of the skin and around the mouth from drooling should be kept clean.

The French Bulldog does have a few unique characteristics that an owner needs to keep in mind and be aware of at all times. We will review those in more detail.

They tend to be very sensitive to heat. Short faced dogs do not have the ability to pant as efficiently as other dogs and that is what keeps them cool. Owners of French Bulldogs need to minimize outdoor activity on hot days to prevent heat stroke. Proper shade and water should always be nearby.

Also, due to their flattened snout they have the tendency to snort, wheeze, grunt and snore at night. Some will also drool excessively. Finally, because they take in a lot of air when they eat, they can be a gassy dog (the air has to go somewhere!).

A quick word of caution regarding swimming pools and French Bulldogs—they don't do well together. Because of their boxy build and heavy head, most cannot swim and could drown in a swimming pool.

Common health concerns include eye problems, brachycephalic syndrome, disk disease, allergies, and hip dysplasia.

Despite these concerns French Bulldogs are fun, sociable and entertaining pets with few faults. They thrive on human contact and make every effort to please their family. With a life span from 12 to 14 years, they will make a fine companion for a long time.

New French Bulldog Puppy Supplies You Must Have

If you are bringing home a new French Bulldog puppy there are certain puppy supplies you must bring home with you.

A new French Bulldog puppy is very cute and the decision to bring one home is often emotional, but you can't forget there are certain things you must have.

The move away from its mother and litter mates can be difficult at first for the new puppy. If you want that transition to be as smooth as possible here are the correct puppy supplies you must have. Use this as a new puppy checklist.

It is best to obtain these puppy supplies before bringing your new best friend home. Once the new puppy is home things can get very hectic.

First make sure you have two bowls. One bowl will be for water and the other will be for the puppy's food. The best type of bowl is stainless steel. These will not chip or crack like glass, ceramic or even plastic. This is really a completely separate topic, but be sure to feed your new puppy the same food it has been eating for the first few days and slowly add a well selected dry kibble type puppy food over the next couple of weeks.

A pet gate is also a must have puppy supply item. Be sure to designate an area where the puppy can safely roam free and close of this area with a puppy gate, also called an indoor dog gate. Make sure this area has nothing the new puppy can chew on that will be hazardous.

Every puppy needs something to chew on that belongs to them. It is in their nature to chew-so make sure you give your new dog a chew toy that will satisfy their needs. If you do not give them something that they know is okay to chew they will find something else and that won't make you very happy.

Your new French Bulldog will need a bed. Often for the first few weeks a box with blankets or towels will work very well. The puppy will prefer to sleep in an area where it feels secure, so don't make the bed area too big. As the dog grows then it will be time to invest in a nice bed, but wait until it gets through the chewing stage first.

A hot water bottle and a ticking clock can often be a pretty decent substitute for the pup's mother. Put this in the bed area and that should help with the new transition at east for the first few days.

A collar and leash for your new French Bulldog is a good idea. Just make sure the collar is adjustable so it doesn't grow out of it too fast. The earlier in its life you can introduce a collar and leash is a very good idea. For this breed of dog a harness collar is best. There will be more on this in a later chapter.

If you are going to be crate training your new puppy you will need a crate. The crate needs to be a size that will accommodate the puppy when it is full grown. So keep that in mind. This will be where your puppy sleeps.

Something else you should also consider is pet insurance. Your new dog will have accidents and become ill just like a human. Pet insurance makes going to the vet very inexpensive and in the long run your pet will receive better care throughout its life.

Best Ways to Puppy Proof Your Home or Apartment

Keeping your new French Bulldog puppy safe is very important.

Bringing a new French Bulldog puppy home to roam around is just like having a little infant child that just learned to walk. They like to explore and get into everything. As a result you must do things to make your house puppy safe. Here's what to do to make your house safe for your puppy.

You should puppy proof your home well before you bring your new pet home. By having your home prepared for the new arrival you will insure its safety and prevent emergencies that could be life threatening.

First you need to decide where in your house the puppy will be allowed walk about. It is a good idea to put up barriers so certain areas are off limits and there is no worry of your new best friend going where it shouldn't.

Now that you have a designated area for the puppy you need to inspect it carefully for anything that may cause problems.

The best way to do this is to look at your house from the puppy's perspective. Crawl around and look at everything that might seem enticing to the new pup or pose a hazard.

French Bulldog Puppies are naturally very curious and will get into just about anything that is on the floor or within their height. Electrical cords or telephone cables need to be removed or taped higher than the new puppy's reach. If a puppy chews into an electrical cord it can be lethal or they can get very serious burns. They can easily get tangled in phone cords and possibly strangle.

Take caution to remove anything that might be on low areas like coffee tables. Small decorative pieces, books, magazines--anything of this nature should be removed from the table as it might look good to chew or could fall off.

As you crawl around looking for objects, look for anything that might be small enough that could be chewed or even swallowed that could pose a hazard just as it would for a small child.

French Bulldog puppies love to chew. It is in their nature so there isn't much you can do to stop that. Be sure to remove anything they could get to that they should not be chewing. You should leave them appropriate chew toys designed for puppies, however.

Keep in mind that puppies love to swallow what they chew. Why just the other day, while watching television, there was a story about a family that kept losing their baby pacifiers. They had a feeling their new puppy might be chewing them-but they didn't think it was possible that it could be swallowing them. The dog was taken to the vet and x-rays showed it had 15 pacifiers in its stomach! Now of course, if you are like me you may be wondering, new baby....new puppy... hmmmm... what was that family thinking? But that's a whole different story.

There are many house plants that are not good for puppies. As a good rule of thumb, remove all house plants from the areas where the new puppy will roam.

You should also make sure that all household cleaners are stored outside of the puppy's reach. Many items like: insecticides, mothballs, antifreeze, fertilizers, insect poisons, and rat poisons can be fatally dangerous to dogs.

If the new puppy will be allowed to roam in the bathroom, be sure to keep the toilet lid down. Many cleaners used to keep the toilet bowl sanitized can be dangerous.

In summary, the best way to puppy proof your home is to do it crawling around from their perspective. Look for low hanging objects and keep in mind: anything that could be harmful to a small child could also be bad for your new French Bulldog puppy.

How to Socialize Your French Bulldog Puppy

<u>This is the most important chapter</u>

<u>you will read in this book.</u>

The first three months for puppies is the most important time in their life. This is the window of time in a puppy's life that determines the type of dog they will become as an adult. Proper socializing for your French Bulldog puppy is most critical during this time. This is when the dog's future temperament, character and behavior habits will be developed.

What you do right and what you do wrong with your puppy during this time period will affect their behavior forever.

A properly socialized French Bulldog puppy will grow up to be well adjusted, obedient, trustworthy, non aggressive, easier to train and an overall better companion.

French Bulldogs that have not been socialized properly can have a very different path in life. They will have trouble adapting to new situations, new people, and new challenges. They are more likely to be fearful, stressed and have difficulty with learning and training. In addition, they usually have more behavior problems like biting, chewing, barking, digging, aggressiveness and more. Even simple activities like going to the vet can be a nightmare.

Experts agree that proper socialization of puppies during the right time in their life has a bigger influence on their behavior as an adult dog that their particular breed.

It is important to know that socialization must be done during this time period. It is not something you can catch up on later. Yes, it is possible to attempt socialization with a puppy later in life, but the job is much, much more difficult and will produce only limited results.

So how do you properly socialize your French Bulldog puppy?

Well, that actually begins with a puppy the minute they are born. The mother of a puppy begins the socialization process. She does this in many ways through sight, sound and smell. She massages with her tongue to stimulate a puppy's elimination and clean them. She also will give a puppy their first lessons in discipline.

A puppy's liter mates also have a very important role in socialization. They learn from each other as they play and interact together.

For these first two reasons it is important puppies not leave their mother and litter mates until they are 8 weeks old. If they leave to early they will miss all of the early socialization learning that can only happen by being with the mother and litter mates.

From 8 weeks to 13 weeks (give or take) is this critical window when you will be in charge of the socialization process.

During this time you will be exposing your French Bulldog to as many situations as possible that are controlled, safe and non-threatening.

It is very important to keep in mind as you expose your puppy to new people, other animals, objects, sights, sounds and different situations that this be done in a manner where it will be safe and they will not be scared. If a puppies first experience with something is frightening or painful it will defeat the purpose. It can result in a phobia of that experience and you don't want that. So take it slow and always be reassuring. Keep the sessions short so your puppy will not be overwhelmed.

As well, take care not to expose your puppy to potentially aggressive dogs or dogs you do not know. Make sure children that the puppy is exposed to are gentle and not rough. To safe guard from disease, because puppies are not completely vaccinated at this age, do not exposed to any animals that may be sick or have not been properly vaccinated themselves.

Proper socialization involves stimulating all five senses of your puppy. It is the introduction and desensitization to the sounds, tastes, sights, smells and touch they will experience every day of their life. It will prepare a puppy with how to deal with most all situations they will encounter in an appropriate manner.

The best place to start is between you, your family and your new puppy. In a safe, gentle and loving manner hold your puppy, stroke its belly, and touch it all over while talking to it. Invite other family members and friends you know and trust to do the same.

Invite your friends to bring their healthy and vaccinated dogs, puppies, even cats to your home to meet and play with your new French Bulldog puppy.

Involve your new puppy in everything you do. Make sure this is always under close supervision. Make sure it is involved with all the daily routine of your house. You want it to be comfortable in its new environment. Allow your puppy to explore your home inside and out.

As much is possible take your puppy with you where ever you go. Carry it to parks, schools, playgrounds, shopping centers, places where there will be crowds of different people.

Take your puppy for short trips in your car or truck. If you have a boat, take it on boat rides.

When you expose your puppy to loud sounds it is best to do this at a distance first, so it is not scared. Eventually you can bring is closer.

During this time also expose your puppy to care and grooming activities like bathing, brushing, inspecting tail and ears, clipping of their nails.

Give your puppy suitable chew toys and play games together.

Always be mindful of how your puppy is reacting to the new situation. You want your puppy to take things at its own pace. Never force or rush your puppy into something it does not seem ready for. Your puppy will have a short attention span and also tire quickly. Don't do too much at one time.

It not recommended you put your puppy on the ground where unknown animals may have access to during this time period. Once your puppy has been complete vaccinated it will be safer to do this.

Also, once the final vaccines are completed it is a good idea to enroll in a puppy school. That way, your French Bulldog puppy will continue to get further socialization with dogs their own age in a controlled environment.

How to Teach Your Puppy its Name

One of the first things you will need to do with your new French Bulldog puppy is to give it a name. After that you will need to teach your puppy its name. Here is the best way to do that.

There is much that needs to be done with a new puppy in its first couple of months after coming to your home. If it knows its name everything will go smother and training will be faster. Many people feel that just by using a puppy's name it will catch on and this is true to a certain extent. But that takes longer than if you were to have a focused training effort.

Training your French Bulldog puppy to learn its name is not hard.

First you should choose a location that is quiet and without distractions. You do not want to do this training in the middle of the kitchen or living room where there is lots of activity (at first).

Also, keep in mind your puppy has very little patience and a short attention span. For the training to be most effective, keep the sessions short—no more than 5-10 minutes at the most.

Say your puppy's name in a high pitched and happy tone. Your puppy will be able to sense your emotions even at an early age. If you are happy your puppy will be happy and you want the name association to be positive and happy.

What you want is to have your puppy look at you and make eye contact when it hears its name called out.

Every time you say your puppy's name and it looks up at you and makes eye contact praise your puppy and give it a treat. Continue to do this over and over again, always giving a treat and lots of praise at first.

The next phase of this training is to do this in areas where there is a little activity or slight distraction and some noise perhaps. As your puppy progresses, continue the training in areas where the activity, distraction and noises continue to increase. Also, back off on the treats and offer them as a reward only occasionally. But do offer lots of praise every time.

Make sure you use your puppy's name only in positive situations. You always want your puppy to associate its name with good things in mind.

How to Win Your Puppy's Respect

When you first bring a new French Bulldog puppy into your home the natural tendency is to lavish upon it lots of attention and affection because it is so cute. Whatever the new puppy wants it seems to get. That is okay but, only to a certain extent.

It is important to welcome the puppy into your home in a way that is comfortable and loving, but you should not go overboard. You do not want to always let the puppy have its way.

If the puppy gets too much attention and everything it wants it can grow up to be spoiled and have no self control and no self discipline. Most important it will have no respect for you.

If your puppy has no respect for you it will have no reason to obey you or do anything for you.

Before any training can begin with you puppy it must respect you.

Your French Bulldog puppy, which will soon become a grown dog, needs a leader and that leader must be you. It you do not assume a leadership role your dog will think it is the leader and that will be a real problem. As you assume the role of leader in the hierarchy you can start the process of developing respect.

Respect is not something that can be forced into your puppy. It must be earned. The best way to earn respect is by teaching a few basic training commands, being consistent and dealing with negative behavior in the right way.

If you want your puppy to respect you it must trust you, and one of the best ways for this to happen is if you are consistent in how you engage with your puppy. If your puppy comes to learn what to expect from you it will trust you more and respect will follow.

Here is an example:
When your puppy engages in negative behavior like barking, whining, biting, jumping up it is important you handle the situation with consistency. Always have the same reaction and response to the behavior, so your puppy will not be confused. Be sure to give praise for good behavior.

One of the most effective ways to teach that negative behavior is unacceptable is to pay no attention to it. You want your puppy to know that when it engages in bad behavior it will not get attention from you. If you show a reaction, quite often, that is exactly what the puppy wants. React to and give praise for only good behavior, that way your puppy will learn to respect you.

As early as possible you want to start training your French Bulldog puppy. This will further develop its respect for you. Teach it basic commands like "sit" and "no" at first. In a later chapter there is more on how to teach these commands. When your puppy successfully accomplishes what you want with these commands offer praise and small treats.

Feed your puppy at regular times and those times should be when you decide

—not when your puppy decides. As well, it is best if you do not eat at the same time. In dog packs, the Alpha, or leader dog, eats first. If your puppy eats before it gets the chance to see you eat first it will think it is the leader.

When playing with your puppy always show that you are in control. You should be the one that that initiates the beginning and the ending of play time; it shows that you are in control.

The first few months of a French Bulldog puppy's life are very important in their development. This is the time you should be executing the above suggestions so that your puppy learns to respect you from the very beginning and grows into a well mannered and obedient dog.

How to Teach Your Puppy to Sit, Stay and Come

Learning how to sit, stay and come are the three most important commands your French Bulldog puppy will learn. Your puppy should be taught these obedience commands as soon as it knows its name. Knowing these will help it to both be well mannered and for safety.

This chapter will be broken down into three parts. The first part will focus on the best way to teach how to sit, the second part will teach how to stay and in the final section you will learn how to train your French Bulldog puppy to come when it is called.

As with all training, because puppies have a very short attention span, remember to keep the sessions short, 5-10 minutes at the most. Also, you need to have patience and be consistent with your training. Work at it every day and always keep it positive. Obedience training should be a fun and bonding experience for the both of you. It is important your puppy looks forward to this time.

How to Teach the "Sit" Command

Make sure you have a pocket full of small pieces of treats you will offer as a reward for a job well done.

It is best to do this in an area that is quiet and there are no distractions.

Stand so you are facing your puppy and hold a piece of treat in front of its nose. Allow your pup to start nibbling on the treat. As your puppy is nibbling slowly raise your hand until it is just out of reach. Now to get the treat your puppy will have to raise its head and shoulders and the hind end should naturally lower. As soon as a sitting position is reached you should say the word "Sit". Then offer praise and give your puppy another piece of a treat. Continue to do this over and over again.

If your puppy's bottom does not lower to the ground you can help a little by gently touching its back and coaxing the behind down. You can say "Sit" while doing this. Do not force it. Keep repeating the process.

As your puppy progresses, continue this process but do it in areas where there at first a few distractions and then more and more.

How to Teach the "Stay" Command

Teaching your puppy to stay is the next logical obedience command that follows.

While your puppy is in the "Sit" position and you have given a treat put your open palm out in front of its face and say "Stay". If it stays in a seated position for few seconds praise your puppy and reward with a treat. If your puppy moves, have it sit first, then repeat the stay command and hand action. Only reward with praise and a treat when your pup stays in one place for a few seconds. If it does not stay do not punish or show frustration—just do not offer a reward or praise and start over.

The next step is to take a single step away and have your puppy remain in the "Stay" position. Repeat over and over again. Progress by adding a few more steps away and expect a longer and longer time to sit in the "Stay" position. Be sure to reward with praise and treats after each success.

As with the other training sessions you should do this in areas where the distractions are slight at first and then continue to increase gradually.

Eventually your puppy should be able to sit and stay for several minutes while you are standing at a distance.

How to Teach the "Come" Command

Once you have taught "Sit" and "Stay", it is time for your puppy to learn the "Come" command. Teaching this command should come easily for a sitting French Bulldog puppy.

After your pup has been in the sit and stay position for the period of time you want say this command in an enthusiastic voice. When you are ready call out "Come" and hold a treat out in front of you. In most cases your puppy will eagerly come to you to retrieve the new treat. Praise your puppy and give it the treat. It is a good idea that you train your pup to sit again when it comes to you.

If your dog gets up and runs to you without first hearing the come command, say 'No'. Give it no treat or praise and have it return to the spot and start over with sit and stay. Do not be mean or harsh, just firm. Especially, do not show or become frustrated. Your puppy will sense this and it will cause confusion.

As before, start this in an area free of distractions and continue the training in areas where the distractions progressively increase. Eventually you should be able to leave the room, so you are not even within eye sight of your French Bulldog puppy and it will stay until you call out the "Come" command.

How to Stop Puppy Whining

Whining is one of the primary ways a puppy uses to communicate. As annoying as it may sound it is a perfectly natural behavior for a young French Bulldog puppy. Whining is one of the first things a new born puppy learns. It is how they get attention from their mother. When the puppy is hungry it whines and the mother feeds it. The puppy learns very early on that whining produces results.

But now that the puppy is in your home, away from its mother, it must learn to keep whining to a minimum.

Before we can work to stop a puppy from whining, we must understand the reasons it may be whining in the first place.

Why Do Puppies Wine?

Puppies will whine for a variety of reasons and you must know what to look for each time it is whining if you are going to solve and stop it.

First puppies will whine to seek your attention. This happens quite often when they are left alone at night or during crate training. This is the way they share their dissatisfaction when experiencing separation anxiety.

Puppies will also whine when they are hungry or thirsty.

They whine when they are uncomfortable. Perhaps they are too hot or too cold, or maybe they have to go to the bathroom or are afraid. Maybe they are in pain.

If they need to be exercised or want to play a bored puppy will whine.

How to Stop the Whining

When puppies whine it is for a reason; they are trying to tell you something.

The best way to stop puppy wining is to anticipate their needs and take care of them before the whining begins. This also shows that you are in charge and not the puppy. Make sure your puppy has enough food and water and gets plenty of play time and exercise daily. Take them out often to go to the bathroom.

Make sure the area where they sleep is kept clean, dry, warm and safe.

It is very important, unless your puppy is in pain to not respond when it whines. If you have taken care of all its needs and you are certain it is not in pain—do not pay any attention to your pup when it whines. Your puppy needs to learn that, for the most part, whining does not get a reaction from you. In order for this to be successful, everyone in the family must do the same.

The biggest challenge with puppy whining will come at night when it feels separated from you. Your puppy is used to sleeping and being in the pack with its litter mates. When your puppy is separated from you it does not think you are coming back and it will whine. You need to reassure your puppy that you are not going to leave it permanently, just for a while.

To train your French Bulldog puppy that temporary separation is okay try this:

Put your puppy in a crate where it will sleep or another room and leave it alone for a short period of time. Return and give it praise for being good. Do not return if it has whined, only return if it has been quiet.

Continue to do this over and over, leaving it for longer and longer periods of time. Each time you return the puppy will learn that you are indeed coming back and not leaving it for good.

You can place suitable puppy toys in the area with it when you leave so it has something to do. This lets the puppy know the area is a social and fun place too.

If the whining at night becomes excessive, you can try putting a ticking alarm clock in the bed area or an article of your clothing with your scent on it. You can also bring the puppy's bed into your room for the first few nights.

Giving your French Bulldog ample exercise during the day will wear it out and this will help minimize the whining it does at night.

The best advice, as hard as it may seem, is to just ignore it. When your puppy does quiet down, reward that behavior with a short visit and praise.

There may be occasions when you need to respond to whining. If your puppy seems to whine out of the ordinary for a reason other than those we have covered, it may really be in distress. If it whines when it is going to the bathroom, or when it is eating, or when you touch it in a certain spot that can be a problem requiring the vet. That is whining not to be ignored.

How to Stop Your French Bulldog Puppy from Biting

There are many schools of thought on how to stop puppy biting. It is true that puppies will bite or nip instinctively and your French Bulldog puppy will be no different. But a puppy should always be taught that this type of behavior is not acceptable. It always starts out as fun, but needs to be controlled to avoid ongoing problems. The question is what is the best method for your puppy? Here are the steps I have found work best.

A fundamental rule in puppy training and this holds especially true for teaching a French Bulldog puppy how not to bite, is that acceptable behavior should be encouraged and unacceptable behavior should be discouraged. Always keep that basic premise in mind.

When a puppy bites or nips you should ever hit or slap them in the face. This will not work and will more than likely only result in bigger problems. Your puppy may think you are just playing or worse become afraid of you. You want your puppy to respect you, not be scared of you.

Another thing to keep in mind is that whatever method you chose to use to stop biting, you must be consistent. Everyone that comes in contact with the puppy must use the same method. That way the puppy will not become confused.

Puppies actually start learning how to not bite from their mother and litter mates. You will be just continuing this process in similar fashion.

The first thing you can do to stop biting is to yell "ouch" or "no" in a high pitched, loud voice. This is similar to the bark its mother or litter mates would do. You want to startle your pup and let it know you have been hurt. The puppy will sense your emotion and the bite should lighten up. When the puppy lets go praise it.

Don't try and pull your hand from your puppy's mouth because instinctively it will just bear down harder.

When your puppy bites understand that it is being done for a reason. Puppies love to chomp down on everything, unfortunately even your flesh. Redirecting them to a suitable chew toy after you have let out a loud yell is often all that is needed for small puppies.

If biting is persistent spraying your hands with a foul tasting product like Bitter Apple for Dogs can be an effective method. If you don't like the smell on your hands spray it on a pair of gloves and wear the gloves when you play with your puppy. When it bites down and gets an unpleasant taste every time, it will soon learn that biting your hand doesn't taste very good.

In all cases when playing with a puppy after it bites and you take an action stop the play and leave the puppy. You want it to learn that if it bites play time is over.

Another method for extreme cases suggests using a plastic spray bottle filled with water and spraying the puppy in the face every time it bites.

Every day, especially starting when your French Bulldog puppy is young, you want to put your hand in and around its mouth. You want your puppy to learn you will not hurt it, that your actions are to be trusted, that you have full rights to its mouth and that biting is not allowed. This is not suggested for children, but best for adults who will command more respect from the puppy.

In very extreme cases, with an over aggressive puppy or dog, where biting cannot be controlled, it may require professional help. It is best to get help sooner rather than later, because the biting will only get worse.

How to Stop Your Puppy from Jumping

A dog that jumps on you when you come home or on every guest that enters your home can be annoying and embarrassing. This is a behavior that can be trained out of the dog, but it is easiest accomplished when in the puppy stage.

French Bulldog puppies are very excitable and it is in their nature to greet people by jumping on them. (Although they won't jump very high because of their short squatty build, they will still jump.) You can't blame them, they are just happy to see you and your guests. And a puppy is so cute most everyone is okay with it. However, if this type of behavior is allowed it tells the puppy that it is acceptable and it will continue when they become a bigger and heavier dog.

The biggest challenge you will have here is achieving consistency with everyone that your puppy greets. You must ask everyone to not allow your puppy to jump on them, even if they say it is okay. Part of the training here is for people as well as your puppy! If you are trying to do something and your guests do something different your puppy will become confused.

First, it is important to understand why puppies jump. It is because they are social animals and are happy and excited to see people. But they must learn to contain that excitement and not jump on people when they are greeting them.

They best way to help them calm down is if you greet them calmly. They have the tendency to mimic your emotion and will be excited if you are excited and tend toward calm if you are calm.

The other action that needs to take place is if you are jumped on by your puppy; do not pay any attention to it. Ignore your puppy if it jumps on you. If you react when it jumps it is getting some attention from you and that only reinforces what it is doing as correct.

If the jumping persists be stern and tell your puppy "OFF". Never push or kick or hit your puppy with a knee to get it off. Then calmly walk away and ignore it. When your puppy settles down go over and give it praise. You want to show attention and reward good behavior and the opposite for behavior that is unwanted.

It is important to not allow jumping when you are playing with your puppy also. If your pup starts to jump when playing with it give a stern "OFF and stop the play session. Walk away so they know that type of behavior has ended the fun. Return to resume play when it is calm.

To stop your French Bulldog puppy from jumping on guests there are a couple of methods that work well. If you have taught the sit and stay command, you can have it go to an area away from the door where it will sit and stay until you allow it to greet the incoming guest. Ask your guests to please ignore your puppy when they first come in, because you are trying to train it.

If your puppy has not yet learned those commands, put a short leash on it. Have your puppy sit in a spot and stay there until it is calm and you decide the time is right to greet your guests. The leash will help to restrain them. When your puppy is calm be sure to praise it, which will continue to reinforce the acceptable behavior. It is best if your goes over to the puppy and greets it.

With all of these suggestions know that results come slowly. It is important to be patient and be consistent. Also, make sure that everyone in the family follows the same training method so your puppy will not become confused.

How to Introduce a Collar and Leash to Your French Bulldog Puppy

Puppy collar and leash training is very important and should be started early in your new puppy's life. Training your French Bulldog puppy to happily accept wearing a collar and walking on a leash is not the easiest thing to do. There is a right way and a wrong way. Here is the right way to train your puppy quickly to accept a collar and leash.

Here are two very important starting tips:

- The attention span of a French Bulldog puppy is very limited. Training sessions need to be short. As soon as you see their attention wane it is time to stop and move on to something else.
- As a trainer you will need to have patience and the training needs to be done gradually, in stages.

The first thing to do is to buy a collar. Make sure the collar will fit snug enough so the pup cannot wiggle out of it. The collar should also be adjustable so it isn't grown out of too fast.

Because French Bulldogs have short, sensitive necks a normal collar can cause breathing problems and hurt their throat. For that reason a harness collar is best suited for French Bulldogs. This type of collar more evenly distributes any stress and focuses more around their chest than neck.

When you first put the new collar on our dog it should not hurt, but will be foreign and uncomfortable. There will be squirming and whining. Expect this, it is natural. It is best to ignore this behavior while it gets used to the collar. One tip is to give your puppy a toy which will become a welcome distraction while getting used to the new item around its neck.

Once it has learned to accept the new collar and are showing signs of comfort with it, then it is time to start introducing the leash.

Many people ask, what is the best age to start puppy leash training? The most common answer is around 8-10 weeks.

The beginning stages of leash training should all be done in the comfortable and controlled environment of your home-not outside.

The first step is to simply click the leash to the collar and let your pup drag it around for a few minutes each day. Stay close so you make sure it does not get caught up on anything.

If they start to chew on the leash buy one that is a chain version. Just make sure it is not too heavy.

If your dog appears to be afraid of the leash, place it next to their food dish when you are not training. That way your puppy will get used to it and learn it is not something that will cause harm or to be afraid of.

Eventually you can pick up the leash and begin walking around the inside of your home with your dog. Just make sure the leash does not get taut at this point. Also do not try to direct where they walk yet. Do this over the next few days. Remember it is a gradual process.

The next step is to begin walking with the leash attached and directing where the pup should go. Do this at first in the confines of your home. After a few days you can move outside. There are more specifics on this in the next chapter.

When you first go outside for puppy leash training you want to do this in an area where there are the fewest distractions. A backyard, if available , works great. Keep the training short.

Remember when you are puppy training, praise your dog when they do something correct. They want to please you and respond very well to this.

Over time you will be able to take walks with the leash attached in outside areas that have more and more distractions. If you have taken the puppy leash training slow and methodical, if it has been fun and you have rewarded good behavior your new best friend should be well introduced to the leash and collar at this point.

How to Teach Your French Bulldog Puppy to Walk on a Leash

Once your French Bulldog puppy is familiar and comfortable with its collar and the leash being attached it is time to start training how to walk on the leash properly.

The goal here is that the leash should always be slack when you are walking your puppy.

First pick a side you want your puppy to walk on. It really doesn't matter, whatever you are comfortable with, just stick to it.

You want your puppy to be calm when you start leash training. This is best accomplished by having your pup start off in a sit position.

You should start this training in a confined area like the inside of your home or fenced yard. It should be free from distractions.

The two most predominant problems you may encounter when leash training is that your puppy may not want to budge or it wants to lead and pull you.

If your puppy doesn't budge when you start walking with the leash attached simply drop the leash and take a few steps forward. Your puppy, because it is naturally social, will want to be with you and will more than likely follow you. When it does give it a treat and praise. Now pick up the leash and walk forward with your puppy. If it goes with you, (that is what you want), stop after a couple of steps and give your puppy a treat and praise. If it budges again, just like before drop the leash and walk forward.

Keep repeating whatever action you need to get the desired results. Pretty soon your pup will get the idea what is the expected behavior. Just take it slow, be patient and offer lots of praise when it makes accomplishments, no matter how slight.

If your puppy pulls ahead while on the leash, the solution is to simply stop walking. It is not recommended to pull back on the leash to correct this behavior, at least while in the puppy stage. That is negative and you do not want anything negative to be associated with being on the leash. Also that can hurt the puppy's neck and even damage the throat.

When your puppy pulls ahead and you stop you are sending a message. The message is that pulling on the leash is fruitless and does not work. After holding the stop for a second so the message sinks in, call your puppy to you in an enthusiastic voice, switch directions a little and begin walking forward again. Make a game of it. French Bulldog puppies like games, because they are fun.

If puppy pulls ahead again just stop as before. Keep this up until the desired behavior is figured out.

When your puppy does walk with a loose leash give it a treat and offer praise, every so often, so it knows it is doing what you want.

How to Crate Train a French Bulldog Puppy

There are many benefits to crate training your French Bulldog puppy. If used properly a crate can help with house training. It can also become an area where your puppy feels safe, secure and relaxed. This is where your puppy will sleep and travel in.

Crate training should begin right away for French Bulldog puppies, normally at 8 weeks or as soon as they have been weaned and are separated from their mother.

The size of the crate should be large enough to accommodate the puppy when it grows into a full size dog. During the puppy stage it is recommended to use dividers to block off the extra space in the crate. The space available should be just big enough for the puppy to stand up and turn around.

The crate should be kept in a room of your house where there is a lot of activity. You want the puppy to still feel like it is a part of the family and see what is going on. Being in the crate should be a pleasant and desirable experience for your puppy. Put a blanket, towel or bedding in it so it is comfortable and put toys in it so it is fun.

To create a positive association with the crate you will need to coax your puppy into it at first using toys or a treat. "Kong: toys work especially well for this because they filled with something the puppy likes and it will keep them busy for while chewing and licking on it while they are getting used to their crate.

Do not force the puppy into the crate. Go slow at first. You do not want under any circumstance for the puppy to associate the crate with anything negative

At first do not shut the door of the crate. You want the puppy to just get used to going inside a little.

Inside the crate is a good place to feed your puppy. That way it will stay in the crate longer and again associate it with something positive—food.

Eventually you will be able to close the door to the crate with your puppy inside. Only keep the door closed for a minute or two at first. Then go for longer periods of time, like five or ten minutes, and then open and let your puppy out. Gradually you can leave your puppy in the crate for longer and longer periods of time with the door shut.

Eventually you can train your puppy that it is okay in the crate with no one in the room. You will want to start leaving the room, again for very short periods of time and then gradually stay away longer and longer.

This is very important. It is likely the puppy will whine at first when being introduced to the crate. It will think you are going to abandon it and never return. You do not want it to get a response when it whines. So if it whines you must ignore it. Leave it in the crate and only return and let it out when the whining stops.

When not in use leave the crate door open so the puppy can explore it freely.

Do not leave food and water in the crate. It is okay to feed your puppy in the crate. But remove food and water bowls when finished to avoid spilling.

Praising your puppy for not whining and having good behavior is very important; do not forget to do it all the time.

A crate can be very helpful in house training and help to keep your puppy safe. When puppies are young they need to eliminate frequently: after they eat, after play time, after they wake up—just about every hour. If you take your puppy out of the crate and to the place where you want them to eliminate they will learn what you expect of them. You need to be consistent and patient.

Do not expect your puppy to walk to the place where they are to eliminate. For the first several times (days or even weeks) you should carry it from the crate to where it will go to the bathroom.

For the most part dogs and puppies will not eliminate where they sleep, which will be the crate. So this can be very effective in helping the house training part of their early training.

The crate can also help to keep the French Bulldog puppy safe because as it will provide confinement until it learns the rules of the household, keeping it from chewing and getting into things that could be harmful.

At night it can be helpful to bring the crate into your room. The puppy is less likely to experience separation anxiety if it knows you are close by.

Also, if the puppy is well exercised at night it will be more likely to sleep longer in the crate during the night.

How to Potty Train a New French Bulldog Puppy

It does not need to be difficult to potty train a new French Bulldog puppy. You just have to have patience, understanding, and a designated area where you want them to learn it is okay to go to the bathroom.

House training a French Bulldog can be a little more difficult than other breeds, but it is not impossible.

Keep in mind it is especially sensitive to cold and wet environments. So you need to have a designated area that is covered and close to the door of the house, if possible.

Installing a doggie door is a good idea so they can go in and out quickly when they feel the need to eliminate.

It is important to remember that going to the bathroom is natural for a puppy. Your French Bulldog puppy has a very small bladder and will have to go to the bathroom several times a day and will make mistakes at first.

You should begin potty training the very first day you bring your new puppy home. Keep in mind that they will need to go every time the urge hits them and that is going to happen a lot. So it will be necessary for someone to watch your new best friend as much as possible, at least in the first few days.

Generally speaking your French Bulldog puppy will need to go to the bathroom immediately after it wakes up from a nap, immediately after eating or drinking and after playtime. On these occasions pick your puppy up and take it to the area you want it to use to go potty. If it roams outside of the area just pick it up and bring it back.

When it does go to the bathroom in the right area, praise your puppy. It needs to know it has done a good job. French Bulldog puppies respond very well to positive reinforcement.

Never yell at your puppy for having a mistake (going in the wrong area). Also, never rub your puppy's nose in it. This type of negative reinforcement does not help. It does not teach your puppy where it should go potty.

While they are learning puppies will make mistakes, expect this and be patient. If they do go in the wrong area you will need to clean it up quickly. If the odor remains then puppies will want to go to the bathroom in that spot again and again.

There are many products on the market that are designed to help with puppy urine clean up and remove odors. If you do not have any of these you can always use vinegar and water.

Eventually you should be able to coax your puppy to walk on its own to the area where you want it to go to the bathroom. This will be better than carrying your puppy. You don't want it to get the idea it will always be carried to the correct spot.

All puppies want to please—keep that in mind and the training will go faster. So even thought it has been mentioned before, we will say it again, when your puppy does go potty in the right spot be sure to always praise it.

Here is something to be careful with. Do not take your puppy on a walk with the intention of the walk to be for it to go to the bathroom. It is best that it goes for a walk after it has eliminated in the area where your training has been taking place. If you are not careful some dogs will get the idea that they are supposed to go potty when on a walk and eventually that is the only time they will go. That becomes a big problem for the dog owner. Dogs and puppies should go on walks, but not with the primary purpose to go to eliminate.

If you have the time to pay attention and work with your new French Bulldog puppy and have patience, when it first comes into your home, it should not take much time at all to have it potty trained.

The ABC's of How to Feed a French Bulldog Puppy Properly

Knowing how to feed a French Bulldog puppy properly in its first year is very important. The first year of your puppy's life is when it does the most growing and it will have special nutritional needs. If you want your new best friend to grow up happy and healthy here are the ABC's you need to know on how to feed a French Bulldog puppy properly.

The First Days in the New Home

In the first few days continue feeding your French Bulldog puppy the same food it has been eating where ever it was before. Also, stick to the same feeding schedule. Over the first week to 10 days slowly begin to mix the food you will be feeding it. A good rule is to mix 25% of the new food with the familiar food at first. Then go half and half and finally 75% new food to old before going completely to the new food.

You may find you have to mix the new food with the old even slower if your puppy shows signs of a loose stool or constipation.

What Type of Food will be Best for My New Puppy?

There are three types of food available for dogs: dry (kibbles), semi moist and moist. The dry food is considered best. It contains less water and is not as fatty as the moist foods. It is also more economical.

There are dog food varieties that are specially designed for puppies. They contain the nutrients that are so important for proper development. Be sure to select a food that has protein, carbohydrates, fats, minerals and vitamins.

Should I Give My Puppy Milk?

Milk is an absolute no-no for puppies. Puppies do not have the proper enzymes in their body to digest milk like humans do.

How about Table Scraps?

Feeding a new puppy table scraps is also not a good idea. There are certain human foods that are dangerous for dogs. If a puppy fills up with table scraps then it is not getting the right type of nutrients it needs for healthy development. Human table scraps are high in calories and only teaches your dog bad habits.

How Often Should I Feed My Puppy?

For the first two weeks stick to the same schedule of feeding that was taking place where it was before. After that, you can feed a new puppy three times per day up until it is 6 months. From 6 months to the first year it should be fed twice per day.

Keep in mind that a French Bulldog puppy will need to go to the bathroom shortly after it eats-so be sure to plan this into your schedule.

How Much Should I Feed My New French Bulldog Puppy

Generally speaking the amount of food given to a French Bulldog puppy should be proportional to its weight and size. For example a 4 pound puppy needs 2-3 ounces of food every day. In comparison, an 8 pound pup will need 4-5 ounces per day.

The Importance of Water

Drinking the proper amount of water is very crucial to any puppy's development and it aids in digestion. Puppies need lots of water. Just because you are involved in potty training, don't deprive them of water. Water makes up almost 60% of the puppies weight and is the most important piece of the food puzzle. Make sure your puppy always has plenty of water to drink.

When Should I Switch to Adult Dog Food?

Because puppy food contains special nutrients designed to aid their growth, don't be too quick to jump to full grown dog food to early. Many people do this because puppy food is more expensive. A good time to make the switch is when your puppy reaches about 80-90 percent of their anticipated adult weight. Note: If you have a small breed puppy it may always require a small breed food because of its size, even as an adult.

What Foods are Considered Dangerous to Dogs?

There are actually quite a few human foods that are considered dangerous to dogs and especially puppies. So make sure everyone in the family knows this.

Here is a list of some more common human foods that should not be given to puppies: raw pork, chicken bones, grapes and raisins, onions, chocolate, caffeinated items, macadamia nuts, gum and candy that contain xylitol, alcohol, avocados and yeast dough.

Puppy Training - 7 Most Important Words Your French Bulldog Puppy Should Know

It is never too early to start puppy training. As soon as you bring your new French Bulldog puppy home the socialization and training process should begin. Your French Bulldog puppy wants to please you and will respond to training if you are consistent and patient.

Granted, your puppy is still young, but young is when habits and patterns start to develop that will shape it as it grows. There are 7 very important words every dog should know and understand. Even as a puppy it should be introduced to these words.

French Bulldog puppy training begins with knowing the correct words to use for your new dog. Here are 7 words it should be introduced to.

As you begin puppy training it is important that there is consistency. Everyone that has contact with the new puppy needs to make sure they are using the same words so there is no confusion. Each of these words should also have the same behavior expectation.

1. Your puppy's name is the first word that should be learned. Be positive and encouraging when using the name. You want to puppy to like their name and associate it with feelings of being loved.

2. "No" is a word that is often over used, yet important. In order for your puppy to understand the meaning of the word no, you must catch it in the act of doing something that is not good. Your puppy should associate the word "no" with behavior that is not appropriate.

3. "Down" is another helpful word for a new puppy. Puppies are active and should be taught that jumping up on a person is not tolerated.

4. "Sit" is a helpful word that you can start to use with your puppy early on.

Teaching your puppy to sit is a very basic and helpful command. As you start to get into words like this, keep in mind a puppy will have a short attention span. So be patient with training.

5. "Stay" is the next word that will be helpful to teach your new puppy. Often rewarding with a small, healthy snack will help to reinforce this new word and the behavior that is expected with it.

6. "Come" is a command that indicates you want your puppy to come to you. This is a very important command that every puppy needs to learn.

7. The words "Go Lay Down" can be helpful for puppy training when you want it to be quiet and lay in a certain area. In order for this to work it must know where you expect it to lie down. This should be an area where your puppy feels safe and comfortable. If you are crate training this may be the area where you want your puppy to go lie down. If that is the case, you may want to change the command words slightly.

Remember, in order for puppy training to be most effective everyone in the family must be using the same words for the same behavior expectation. As well, be sure to reward your puppy with lots of love and positive reinforcement.

How to Brush Your Puppy's Teeth

A dog is similar to a human in that their teeth need to be brushed periodically. However, many pet owners do not brush their dog's teeth as often as they should, if at all.

Not brushing a dog's teeth can lead to serious health problems. There is a right way and a wrong way to brush a puppy's teeth. Here is how to brush your puppy's teeth so it will look forward to it every time.

Why Do I Need to Brush My Puppy's Teeth?

When dogs eat they get food particles stuck in between their teeth and along their gum line, just like humans. Dogs are susceptible to many of the same improper mouth hygiene problems as humans. Their teeth need to be brushed regularly or else there will be a build of plaque which can lead to gingivitis, cavities and other teeth problems. Dogs can get tooth aches and even lose teeth prematurely if they are not properly cared for. A dog that has teeth problems will not eat properly and that will affect its health, disposition and demeanor.

When is the Best Time to Start Brushing My Puppy's Teeth?

At about the age of eight to 10 weeks is a perfect time to start brushing a dog's teeth. The earlier in life you can start the better so a healthy habit is established. It will be much easier to train a dog and get them used to teeth brushing as a puppy than when they get older. However it is something you do not want to rush into. You must start the process slowly so they get used to it and are not afraid.

How to Introduce Teeth Brushing to Your Puppy Properly

Brushing your puppy's teeth will be a foreign experience at first. But if you introduce it the right way, you should have no problems.

First you need to get the right tooth paste. You absolutely need to use toothpaste that is made for dogs. Many of these have meat flavors that dogs love and work very well for cleaning teeth. Under no circumstance should you ever brush a dog's teeth with human tooth paste. It can damage their teeth and most dogs will resist the minty flavor of human tooth paste.

Start by putting a small amount of dog toothpaste on your finger. Let your puppy smell and lick the toothpaste. Sometimes you may have to experiment to make sure it likes the flavor. Once you have found one it likes, you are on your way.

For a couple of days just let your puppy smell and lick the paste so it gets to remember the flavor. Then begin putting a small dab up to its lips. Do this for a couple of days.

Now you want to put a small amount of the tooth paste in the front of the puppy's mouth. If it nips at you make a loud, shrill noise that will tell your dog nipping is not acceptable behavior.

After doing just this for a couple of days now you are ready to put the toothpaste on a finger and touch just the front teeth with it. Let your dog lick it all off and enjoy it. After a day or so of this you are ready to spread the tooth paste on the front and back teeth, just enough so it gets the flavor all throughout its mouth.

As you can see this is a slow and gradual process that can take a couple of weeks. But if you are patient and calm and reassuring to your pet it will pay off for you in big ways. If you can brush your own dog's teeth it will save you lots in veterinarian bills down the road.

Now it will be time to introduce the tooth brush. Make sure you have purchased a tooth brush that is designed for your dog breed. At first, put a small dab of the tooth paste on the brush and let your dog smell and lick it off. Do this for a couple of days.

After your pet has become familiar with the tooth brush you are ready to use it. For the first few days only brush the front teeth. The first few times make it quick (5-10 seconds). Gradually increase the time you have the tooth brush in the mouth. Maybe one day just brush the back teeth and the next time brush just the front, mix it up.

You do not want to brush anymore than a minute at a time or else your puppy will not look forward to the event.

How Often Should I Brush My Puppy's Teeth?

The correct answer is as often as you can. You should brush your puppy's teeth daily if possible. If that is not possible it should be done no less than twice per week for the best hygiene care.

Be sure to change the tooth brush often, as soon as it looks like it is getting rough or worn down.

The Right Way to Start Bathing Your New French Bulldog Puppy

There is right way and a wrong way to bath your new French Bulldog puppy. If you go about it the wrong way you may establish a lifetime of horrible behavior when it comes to taking a bath. Here is the right way to give your new French Bulldog puppy a bath.

How Often Should I Wash My Dog?

The first thing you need to know is that dogs do not need to take a bath as often as people do. Once a month, or even every six weeks is usually just fine for your French Bulldog. Bathing your dog too often can actually be harmful. Bathing too frequently can damage their coat and skin and remove their natural oils.

A good rule of thumb is the smell test. If your dog starts to have a dog odor that is too strong, then it is usually time for a bath.

What Type of Shampoo Should I Use to Wash My Dog?

If you are only washing your dog once a month, which is plenty often, you can get away with a mild shampoo. Something like you might use for a baby or child would work, just so long as it is mild. The best is to use a special bathing soap designed for dogs that won't remove their natural oils or damage their coat.

How to Introduce Your French Bulldog Puppy to the Bathtub

Before giving an actual bath to your puppy you should start introducing it to the bathtub and the process before hand. This will help relieve any anxiety and make the event something that does not have to be feared.

Start very basic by using the word "tub". Say the word and then run with your puppy to the bathtub. Touch the bathtub and say the word. Do this several times over a day or so. Don't put your puppy in the tub just yet.

Now place a bath mat at the bottom of the tub. You might even put some puppy toys on the mat. When you say tub this time run to the tub and then place your puppy in the tub. Reward with a treat. Some people even like to spread something like a little peanut butter on the bath mat. Do this for a day or so. Play with the puppy while it is in the empty tub, make it feel comfortable. This should be something fun it looks forward to.

The next step is to run a little warm water with the puppy in the tub. Let it drain for the first few times. The next step is to let the water fill up to about ankle high for your pup. If there is any real anxiety this is where it can happen most significantly. If the puppy squirms or looks uncomfortable offer calming words, perhaps sing to it, say "good dog." The idea is to be calm and reassure that everything is okay.

Eventually you should be able to add enough water to make the bathing process work and your dog will actually enjoy and look forward to bath time.

Puppy Washing Tips

As you wash your puppy, pour the warm water over its body slowly and continue offering reassurance. Start with the rear and work your way forward. It is not a good idea to pour water on the head, at least at first. Just use a wash cloth for the face area and ears. Make sure you have rinsed well so all the soap is removed from the coat.

When leaving the tub your dog is probably going to shake and that can soak both you and the room. To avoid this as much as possible, drain the water and dry our puppy off in the tub before placing it back on the floor. Be sure you have a nice absorbent towel on hand for drying. After drying place the towel on the floor. Many dogs like to roll in the towel to continue drying themselves off.

Helpful Tips on Teething and the Need to Chew For Your Puppy

It is a well known fact that puppies like to chew and your French Bulldog puppy will be no different. The reason they chew is that it is a natural part of teething.

When they are first born puppies have no teeth. But around the time they begin to wean off their mother, around six to eight weeks, their first set of incisors will start coming in. Puppies will grow 14 teeth on the top and 14 teeth on the bottom.

As these teeth come in this can be an uncomfortable and painful period for a puppy. Puppies will chew during this time to ease the pain and to test out the texture of different objects. It is important for their owners to know this need to chew is natural.

Even though these first 28 teeth are called "baby teeth" they are still very sharp. For this reason you should always be careful when your puppy bites and nips at you.

Between three and seven months these baby teeth will fall out and be replaced by 42 permanent teeth. If you see baby teeth on the floor or in the water bowl, don't be alarmed. Some teeth that fall out you may never see, because they may be swallowed by your puppy. Again there is no need for alarm or concern.

As the new teeth are coming in it is a good idea to be checking to make sure a stubborn baby tooth is not refusing to come out and making it crowded for the adult tooth. This is common and should be looked at by a veterinarian if you see it develop in your puppy.

Your puppy will seek out things like shoes, blankets, curtains and anything else they can find to chew on during this period. If this doesn't sound good to you, give your puppy other objects to chew on.

A knotted wash cloth soaked in water and then frozen can be a big help in soothing sore gums. Also, a hard rubber toy called a "kong" can be filled with broth and then frozen. That is also a good idea.

Items Not Suitable for French Bulldog Puppies to Chew On

Rawhide

Though sold in most pet stores, rawhide items should not be given to a dog until they are at least one year old. The developing digestive systems of young puppies cannot always break down rawhide. If a puppy swallows a piece of rawhide, it can damage their throat, stomach, or intestines. Also, puppies tend to swallow rawhide in large chunks which can cause choking.

Pigs Ears

Most dogs love the delicious taste of pig's ears, but they are not for puppies. Again, like rawhide, the digestive system of a puppy is not mature enough to handle this type of a product.

Vinyl Chew Toys

A puppy can chew through one of these in a matter of minutes and they will swallow the pieces along the way. The pieces will take a couple of days to pass through the puppy and this is not a pleasant experience.

Here are Objects Suitable for French Bulldog Puppies to Chew

Latex and Rubber Toys

These are toys that are harder and more difficult for a puppy to break off and as a result there is not as much risk in swallowing large pieces. Along this line are the hard rubber "Kong" toys already discussed.

Nylabones

These can be good chew objects for puppies as they flake off in grain size pieces and easily pass through an under developed puppy digestive system. These bones are often infused with flavor, helping to entice puppies to chew them. There is also a version of the Nylabone that is covered with bumps, which are great for teething puppies.

Rope and Material Toys

French Bulldog puppies enjoy putting items with different textures in their mouths. Many toys incorporate rope, rubber, and sturdy material to satisfy the urge of a puppy to chew many different textures. Some of these toys can even be put into the freezer to help soothe the painful gums of a teething puppy.

One final word: Whenever you give your puppy something to chew on make sure you are always there to supervise so there are no problems, like choking.

Puppy Identification Options

Here is a frightening statistic:

One out of three pets will get lost or stolen during their lifetimes. Even puppies, because of their natural curiosity can wonder off and get hopelessly lost. Without identification 90 percent won't return home.

That is why it is a good idea to consider identification options for your new puppy. With proper identification you will be able to greatly increase the chance of finding your puppy if it has become lost or stolen.

There are three primary methods for identification of puppies today.

Microchipping

Using a microchip as a method for pet identification is the most modern and hi tech concept today. It is becoming very popular and is highly effective. In fact many municipalities are making the change to have this form of pet identification a part of their licensing program.

This process involves the use of a small identification chip that is inserted just under the skin of your puppy, usually in the upper back area. It is small, about the size of a grain of rice. But it can contain very valuable information especially contact details about the puppy's owner.

Today many city pet programs, human society facilities, and veterinarians have equipment that scans and reads information from these micro chips. They operate much like bar scan readers at the grocery store.

For a puppy, the process of having a microchip implanted under the skin of a puppy is similar in how it feels to that of receiving a vaccine injection.

Pet Tag

The more traditional method for identification is the pet tag. This has been the standard for many years and is still required by most cities as part of the licensing process. The benefit of this method is that it is relatively inexpensive and easy to implement. The tag is generally engraved with owner contact information. The drawback of this type of method is that a tag attaches to a collar and if the collar is not worn, there is no means for identification of your puppy.

Tattoos

Tattoos are not just for people. They are becoming more and more popular as a means of identification for pets today. In most cases a tattoo is applied either to the inside of your pet's ear flap or on the inner thigh region. This provides a permanent means of identification. However, it can be a painful procedure requiring anesthetic. The other consideration is that a tattoo can fade or distort over time and become difficult to read. As well, if the owner information ever changes, over the life of your dog that can be a concern with a permanent tattoo.

Puppy Air Travel -The Most Current Guidelines You May Not Know

Pet air travel is growing in the US and around the world. More and more people are traveling through the skies with their pets. However, pet air travel can be tricky. There are certain things that you need to be aware of if you want your puppy to travel with you. Here are guidelines for pet air travel that you need to know.

Many airlines will allow and have provisions for pet air travel. However, each airline may have its own particular requirements or guidelines. So the best advice is always check with your airline first and ask what their requirements are for pet travel.

Some airlines, if the pet is small, will allow you to bring it with you. But the pet must be transported in an airline approved pet carrier. Be sure before you buy a pet carrier that it is approved by the airline that you will be flying with.

There are also companies that specialize in transporting your pet for you. If you want your pet to come with you to your travel destination, but you do not want to be involved in their transport, you can hire a company that will handle all the arrangements for you. They will insure your pet is transported safely and well cared for during the flight. There are many companies like this. They can be found online by doing a simple search using the words: pet air travel.

Whatever type of carrier your pet will be transported in be sure to take the time well before the trip to get your pet comfortable with being in it. A few weeks before the trip, have your pet spend a few minutes in the pet carrier each day so it will get familiar with it. Pets like to be safe and comfortable just like humans. If they are familiar with the carrier they will be using for the trip, that will help to make things go smoother.

Make sure that the carrier has the proper identification tags on it and also any special instructions about your pet that may be required.

On the day of the flight feed your pet well before the flight. A good rule is to feed it 4 to 5 hours before flying. It is advised that 2 hours before the flight give your puppy a healthy drink of water.

Some pets may require a mild sedative for flying. It is always best to consult your veterinarian for this type of help.

When you arrive at your destination your pet will probably need to have a little exercise and go to the bathroom. There is a good chance they will also want food and water soon as well. Be sure you are prepared to provide it this help.

Make sure you have planned in advance how your pet will be transported once you get to your destination. Some forms of transportation do not allow pets. So you want to make sure you have this planned out.

Top 4 Reasons Why You Need Pet Insurance

Having pet insurance for your French Bulldog puppy can be very helpful. It can ensure better health care over its life and can save you a lot of money.

So why don't more people have insurance like this? It is because most people do not understand how this type of insurance can be so helpful. Here are the top 4 reasons why you need pet insurance for your puppy.

Insurance for your pet is something that many people do not know much about and therefore do not have it. That is very unfortunate. For a number of reasons this type of insurance can be very helpful to the health and overall life of your pet and it can save you money.

First of all, obtaining coverage like this is not as expensive as many people think. When you consider how much a trip to the veterinarian can cost, by comparison, insurance is cheap. Insurance companies that carry pet insurance have different policies and different types of coverage, just like for humans. But a general policy that offers pretty decent coverage can cost around $15-$18 per month for a cat and between $22- $28 per month for a dog.

It is estimated that the amount of money that is spent on a dog over a life time is between 10 and 15 thousand dollars. A good portion of that is for bills due for healthcare, illness and accidents. Having pet insurance can save their owners money by covering a lot of these expenses.

The second reason to consider insurance like this is that your dog will receive better health care and will more than likely live a longer and more fit life. Most owners want the best for their pets, right? You are probably no different. However, because of how expensive it is to go to the veterinarian, in many cases the pet is not taken in to the veterinarian for illness or injuries when they should be.

Animals, like humans, get sick, they get diseases and they become injured. For that reason having affordable healthcare for them makes the same kind of sense it does for other members of your family. If you know the expenses will be covered under insurance you will be more likely to take your pet into the veterinarian when it needs help.

Third, many insurance policies like these also cover well visits. If you have insurance that covers well exams you will be more inclined to take your pet in for well exams. Just like for humans preventative medicine is always best.

Well exams will help to catch problems when they are small before they become bigger and possible life threatening.

Fourth, as your dog ages they will need health care more and will be more prone to accidents later in life, just the same as humans. You can greatly help to extend their life and comfort in life, when they will need it most, if you have pet insurance for them. There are even insurance programs that are designed specifically for older pets.

Here is where you can learn even more on Pet Insurance.

How to Teach Your French Bulldog Puppy Tricks

What you will learn here is how to teach your French Bulldog puppy tricks.

Keep in mind that teaching tricks to you French Bulldog will take more time and considerable more patience than with other dog breeds. French Bulldog's can be stubborn, but they can be trained and taught tricks.

Some may disagree that a puppy is too young to teach tricks. But that is not the case. A puppy has a shorter attention span than a full grown dog. That is the important factor you must keep in mind if you are to be successful.

A puppy is very capable and willing to learn. In fact, pleasing their owner is the desire of every puppy. Plus if you teach them dog tricks it will be good exercise which they need for healthy development. It will also help to keep them from getting bored and aid in their behavior. A dog that does tricks is generally a well behaved dog and one that doesn't get into trouble.

There are three things you must keep in mind if you are going to be successful:

Because a puppy has a short attention span as soon as you see them loose interest in the training or game, it is time to stop and move on to something else.

You must make the training fun. If you are having fun, the puppy will detect this and that will help them to have fun also. Puppies are playful by their nature and if you want the puppy to enjoy what you are doing with them—keep it fun.

You must have patience. Don't expect the puppy to learn as fast as you might expect. They will forget, make mistakes and sometimes take what seems like forever to figure it out. Just be patient and keep at it and they will eventually surprise you.

When working with your puppy be careful and aware that you are not placing them in any situation that might be dangerous or harmful. Your puppy will completely trust you.

When your puppy does something correct offer lots of praise. Tell them they are a good dog. Positive reinforcement will really help. That is what your puppy lives for!

If it is possible, you should consider picking the same time each day to work with your puppy. The pup will look forward to that time of day as something that is fun.

Be sure you understand the trick you are going to teach ahead of time. Think it through. Know what you want the puppy to do. Also know how you will show them the expected behavior. Also know the command you will use.

As you repeat the training be consistent and make sure to do the same thing every time, until they figure it out on their own.

It can be helpful when showing what you want it to do by positioning your puppy's body in the correct position. Do this from ground level. It is less threatening and will be more comfortable for your dog.

Remember to be patient, make it fun and keep at it. You will be surprised at how well your best friend will respond and soon be doing all sorts of neat tricks with you.

How to Exercise Your French Bulldog

Your French Bulldog puppy is a breed that does not need a lot of exercise. But make no mistake that does not mean they can go without exercise. It does need some form of exercise and on a daily level.

Getting exercise is vital to your French Bulldog's over well being, health, and temperament and will increase its lifespan.

Exercise for your French Bulldog can take place indoors and outdoors. Though, like any dog, they will prefer outdoors, it is not necessary. Because of their sensitivity to heat, be careful having your French Bulldog outdoors if it is above 85 degrees (29.4 Celsius) for extended periods of time. They will quickly become overheated which can lead to heat stroke.

Be aware that your French Bulldog, although a fun dog, can be prone to laziness and without regular exercise will quickly pile on the pounds. But it does not require a full days worth of activity. A short burst of energetic activity from ½ to 1 hour a day is plenty.

Inside activities for French Bulldog's may include: They love to run, chase and retrieve squeaky dog toys. Many of these dogs enjoy playing with an ice cube on the kitchen floor. You can even play hide and seek with a favorite toy inside.

Outside activities for French Bulldog's may include: a daily walk (weather permitting), playing catch with a tennis ball or tossing a stick. If you have a confined area, like a back yard or patio, just letting your French Bulldog run around outside for a short while taking in all the smells will be adequate.

Vaccines Your French Bulldog Puppy Needs

Vaccinations (sometimes referred to as shots) are given to puppies to help prevent them from contracting diseases and viruses.

Dogs and puppies can contract diseases and viruses in a variety of ways: from direct contact with infected dogs, through contaminated feces, from drinking contaminated water and even insect bites. Many of these diseases and viruses can be life threatening to puppies.

That is why puppies should be kept away from other animals that you are not certain have had their vaccinations until they have received their vaccines at around the 16 week point. This is also why it is not recommended a puppy that hasn't had all its vaccinations be allowed to walk and romp about outdoors.

French Bulldog puppies should start receiving their first vaccination between 5 and 8 weeks of age and then boosters at around 12-16 weeks.

There are a variety of disease preventative vaccines your puppy will need. Exactly which vaccine is needed and timing for when they are given seems to vary from one veterinarian to the next. Some of the variance is due to the location or environment, some is due to local law, the breed and health status of the dog, lifestyle and travel habits and some is veterinarian preference.

That is why it is highly recommended a French Bulldog puppy at around 5-8 weeks should visit a veterinarian so they can share with you what their recommended vaccines and schedule will be for the area where you live.

What follows here is a general overview of the diseases for which there are available vaccines, when your puppy needs the vaccines, and possible side effects.

Canine vaccinations are broken into two groups: core vaccines and noncore vaccines.

Core vaccines protect dogs from rabies, canine distemper, parvorirus and hepititus. It is generally recommended that all dogs get vaccines in this category.

Noncore vaccines protect dogs from lyme disease, bordetella, leptospirosis and coronavirus. The need for these vaccines for these conditions will vary depending on lifestyle and geography.

Distemper

Distemper is a virus similar to measles in humans and it is transmitted through the air. It is almost always fatal to puppies. It is highly contagious. This is one of the first vaccines your puppy will receive at around 8 weeks of age. Generally this is combined with other vaccines as a 4 in one, 5 in one or even 7 to one. It requires boosters periodically throughout the dog's life.

Rabies

Rabies is a dangerous virus that attacks the nervous system and is always fatal to animals. Once this vaccine is administered there is a small likely hood your dog will contract the disease. The rabies vaccination needs to be given to puppies at around 4 months and then every three years through the dogs life. Many states and cities require as a law that dogs receive this vaccine.

Parvovirus

Parvovirus is extremely contagious and your puppy will be vaccinated for this at the eight week point. It is usually part of the combo vaccine. Parvo causes violent vomiting and diarrhea and can be fatal to puppies. It is spread through feces.

Hepatitis

Hepatitis is a disease of the liver that can spread throughout the body. The vaccination for this is also part of the combo vaccine.

Bordetella (Kennel Cough)

If your dog is going to be in kennels and around other dogs frequently, the vaccine preventing Bordetella is recommended. Bordetella is a respiratory secreted bacterium which is easily transmitted by a coughing dog or nose to nose contact. Exposure is most common in boarding and grooming facilities.

Leptospirosis

Leptospirosis is spread through urine and damages the kidneys and can lead to kidney failure.

Coronavirus

The vaccine to prevent this virus is based on the recommendation of your veterinarian. Coronavirus attacks the intestinal lining and can cause gastrointestinal problems.

Lyme Disease

Lyme disease is carried by the bite of an infected tick. The disease can cause malaise, fever, loss of appetite and eventually a chronic arthritis condition. In areas where ticks are prevalent your veterinarian is likely to recommend this vaccine.

It should be mentioned that adverse reactions to vaccines are infrequent, but possible. Generally the side effects are limited to local pain and swelling. But occasionally there can be an allergic reaction. Usually if this is going to happen it will occur soon after the vaccination. A veterinarian can provide more information on this.

In recent years a new option has been developed that can take the place of booster vaccines, especially for diseases such as distemper and parvovirus. This is called a titer test. The titer test measures the amount of antibodies in your dog's blood. It provides an economical method for determining if your dog actually needs certain vaccine boosters. You will want to check with your veterinarian on this as a possible option.

A Puppy's 10 Commandments

Here are the ten things every puppy must have to live a happy, healthy life as told from the point of view of a puppy.

Number 1

Feed me twice a day a good quality food that has all the nutrients I need so I can grow up big and strong. Once in the morning, so I have energy for the day and again at night so I don't beg for table scraps.

Number 2

Keep my water bowl filled at all times. I need lots of water because I am so active. I will drink all day, but never too much—just enough so that I stay properly hydrated.

Number 3

Buy me a toy that is okay for me to chew on. I have the need to chew. It is what puppies with developing teeth do. I don't like getting in trouble for chewing on something that I am not supposed to.

Number 4

Help me get the exercise I need. I am growing and very active. Take me on walks and play with me every day.

Number 5

I need attention and love. Every day pay attention to me. Teach me tricks and things to do so you will be pleased with me and I will receive treats and praise.

Number 6

Be sure to reward me when I do what is right. The more reward I am given for doing what I am supposed to, the more obedient I will be.

Number 7

Provide me with a place to sleep that I know is mine. Make sure it is safe and warm and not too far from you.

Number 8

Teach me where I am supposed to go to the bathroom. I will have to do this several times a day. And be patient with me while I learn and forgiving if I make a mistake or two in those first few days.

Number 9

As I grow I will need friends. Allow me the ability to socialize with other dogs when the time is right.

Number 10

Be sure to take me to the veterinarian for all the shots I will need and a yearly check up. At times I will get sick and possibly injured. Please take care of me and take me to the veterinarian when I need to, no matter what.

Printed in Great Britain
by Amazon